and Dakota Blue Richards) play on the roof of Jordan College (based on Exeter College) in *The Golden Compass* (2007)

OXFORD
FILM LOCATIONS

Setting the Scene

'a city ... steeped in storytelling ... a place where the past and the present jostle each other on the pavement'

The camera pans over domes and spires, cobbled squares and neo-classical pediments... From Harold Pinter's *Accident* (1967) to Harry Potter's Hogwarts, Oxford's ancient and beautiful buildings have appeared in dozens of movies and TV series in the last half-century or so. This guidebook takes you to the city's best-loved sights, whether it's Lyra's college playgrounds, the cloisters where Harry Potter learns about Quidditch, or a lamppost straight out of C.S. Lewis's Narnia.

In recent years, the cast of *Mamma Mia!* have cycled over Oxford cobbles for an irrepressible sequel *Here We Go Again* (2018) and the glowing stained glass of Exeter chapel formed a backdrop for evil sorcery in *Doctor Strange* (2016).

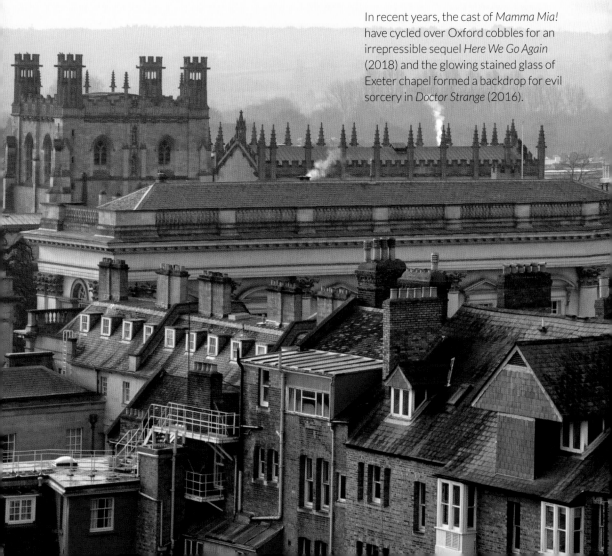

Supercars screeched down ancient Holywell Street in *Transformers: The Last Knight* (2017) while, down the road, Emma Stone and Rachel Weisz starred in *The Favourite* (2018) as rivals for the attention of Queen Anne (Olivia Colman).

Oxford colleges, libraries, chapels and museums have not only been locations for films, they also inspired the original stories – from *Shadowlands*, the story of C.S. Lewis, filmed in the author's college, Magdalen, to *The Golden Compass*, Philip Pullman's Oxford-based fantasy, where Exeter becomes fictional Jordan College. Pullman has called Oxford 'a city ... steeped in storytelling, ... a place where the past and the present jostle each other on the pavement'. Perhaps it is this that makes it such a magnet for filmmakers.

The walks in this book take in some of the city's most delightful and interesting corners and venture out into the nearby countryside, to pubs and palaces, farms and forests. You can, of course, enjoy them without seeing the films. But fans of *Inspector Morse* or *Harry Potter*, *Lord of the Rings* or *Downton Abbey* will find these landscapes full of familiar sights and inspirational places.

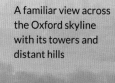

A familiar view across the Oxford skyline with its towers and distant hills

Oxford Inspiration

Stories just seem to pour out of Oxford. The walks in this book explore some of the inspirations and locations associated with Oxford's most famous writers, such as Lewis Carroll and Philip Pullman. C.S. Lewis, who wrote the Narnia books, and J.R.R. Tolkien, author of *The Lord of the Rings*, met over tea in 1926 and grew to be friends, discussing their ideas in a group known as the Inklings, which often met in the Eagle and Child pub.

In the film *Shadowlands* (1993), about the life of C.S. Lewis, Anthony Hopkins played the author, and Debra Winger was his wife, Joy. In *The Golden Compass* (2007), the film of Philip Pullman's novel, Lyra grows up in 'Jordan' College, a fictional institution based on the author's old college, Exeter. Pullman's works are some of the more recent additions to the venerable tradition of stories set and filmed in Oxford, from *Brideshead Revisited* to Morse and beyond. A novel by Nicholas Mosley inspired Harold Pinter's portentous screenplay for *Accident* (1967); it centres on a pipe-smoking, married Oxford don (Dirk Bogarde) in love with his aristocratic Austrian student.

In 1981, the celebrated TV mini-series of *Brideshead Revisited*, based on the novel by Evelyn Waugh, was filmed partly in Hertford, Waugh's old college – even using his old room. Charles Ryder (Jeremy Irons) is supposed to be studying here, while Sebastian Flyte (Anthony Andrews) is at Christ Church. In the 2008 film, Lincoln represents both colleges, while – in both the film and TV series – the Brideshead estate itself is represented by Castle Howard in Yorkshire.

Oxford Blues (1984) was a remake of the 1938 film called *A Yank at Oxford* starring Vivien Leigh and Robert Taylor. Rob Lowe played Las Vegas casino worker Nick Di Angelo, studying at Oxford in the hope of impressing glamorous Lady Victoria – it's packed with recognisable locations, including Oriel College. Not long after filming *A Fish Called Wanda*, Michael Palin was back in town, playing an Oxford don in *American Friends* (1991). Also partly set in the university, *True Blue* (1996) adapts Daniel Topolski's book about a mutiny among the Oxford team training for the Oxford and Cambridge boat race.

Oxford-based author Colin Dexter created the character of Inspector Morse and Dexter's mystery novels became a popular ITV drama. Both as the young detective in *Endeavour* (played by Shaun Evans) and as the original veteran inspector (John Thaw), Morse has solved countless murders in Oxford, as has erstwhile sidekick Lewis (Kevin Whately) in his own spin-off series together with Sergeant Hathaway (Laurence Fox).

A Timeless City

Oxford's formal cloisters and echoing quads have represented a variety of real and fictional schools and the university often pops up in films about education. Equally predictably, this ancient city has attracted a number of classic costume dramas, providing convincingly authentic streets and timeworn buildings.

In Alan Bennett's *The History Boys* (2006), about a lively group of teenagers applying for Oxbridge, the boys visit various colleges for interviews. At the end of *An Education* (2009), Nick Hornby's screenplay, based on Lynn Barber's life story, specifies: 'Swelling orchestral music, wide shot of Oxford spires', then a happy close-up before the camera pulls back to show Jenny (played by Carey Mulligan) 'cycling through the streets of Oxford'.

Oxford doubled as a school for *Young Sherlock Holmes* (1985): the outside of the teenage sleuth's Brompton School is actually Brasenose College, while the inside is Eton. In *Another Country* (1984), Brasenose and the Bodleian Library become the public school where Guy Bennett explores sexuality and politics in a fictional recreation of the life of double agent Guy Burgess. Parts of the BBC's 1979 TV series of *Tinker, Tailor, Soldier, Spy*, with Alec Guinness as Smiley, were filmed in the university. In the expensively produced *Heaven's Gate* (1980), Oxford's Sheldonian building and Mansfield College stood in for late 19th-century Harvard.

The immaculate *Howards End* (1992) had a short scene in Magdalen's magnificent college gardens, and co-opts the inside of the town hall as a

MERTON STREET

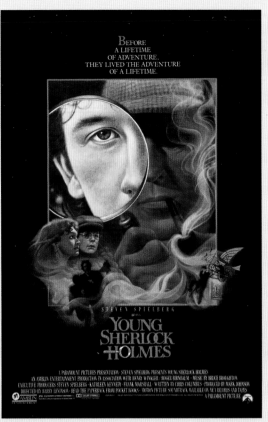

London lecture theatre. The Bodleian's Divinity Hall and neighbouring Broad Street appear in *To Kill a King* (2003), a historical film about Oliver Cromwell, and *The New World* (2005), about Pocahontas, also has scenes outside the Bodleian.

Belle (2013) is the moving story of mixed race Dido Elizabeth Belle, daughter of a former slave and her lover, a Royal Navy Admiral. Parts of Broad Street and cobbled Merton Street, with their timeless Cotswold stone, were used to represent 18th-century London. Gugu Mbatha-Raw, who stars as Belle, grew up in Witney, a market town in Oxfordshire. The popular ITV period drama *Downton Abbey*, actually set in Yorkshire, used several rural locations in the nearby Cotswolds, including Cogges Manor Farm in Witney. In parts of *Colette* (2018), starring Keira Knightley and Dominic West, Cogges Farm stood in for rural France.

Oxford's architecture also serves as a backdrop for the passions and betrayals of Queen Anne's court in *The Favourite* (2018), and *Mary Queen of Scots* (2018), starring Saoirse Ronan and David Tennant, also features scenes shot in Oxford. No doubt the university, stuck – as it sometimes seems – like a butterfly in amber, will continue to provide historical settings for years to come.

PREVIOUS PAGE Oxford's picturesque Merton Street has appeared in *Belle* and other costume dramas

TOP LEFT Christ Church college can be seen behind *The History Boys* on this film poster

TOP RIGHT Brasenose college doubled as the junior sleuth's school in *Young Sherlock Holmes* (1985) starring Nicholas Rowe and Alan Cox

From Bond to Bollywood

Perhaps more surprisingly, Oxford's ancient quads and quaint cobbles have also hosted dynamic action movies and Bollywood dances. While Aston Martins zoom through the quiet streets, Bollywood films fill them with music, dance and glamour. From car chases to musical montages, the city's streets have staged all kinds of cinematic set pieces. So dance – or walk – your own way round the city on these cinematic tours, discovering world famous landmarks and magical secrets.

A Piece of the Action

A Fish Called Wanda (1988), the comic heist movie written by John Cleese, used Oxford's town hall and prison as locations. Pierce Brosnan heads to Oxford as James Bond in *Tomorrow Never Dies* (1997) to 'brush up on his Danish'. In *X-Men: First Class* (2011), Charles Xavier (James McAvoy as a younger version of Patrick Stewart) drinks among iconic Oxford locations.

Mission: Impossible – Rogue Nation (2015) used Blenheim Palace, eight miles north of Oxford, as the baroque setting for a ball. *Doctor Strange* (2016), starring Benedict Cumberbatch, had a mesmerising scene in Exeter College. The 2017 reboot of *The Mummy*, with Tom Cruise, shot scenes outside the Radcliffe Camera and in *Transformers: The Last Knight* (2017), colourful cars speed down Holywell Street.

For 2018's Mamma Mia sequel/prequel *Here We Go Again*, Lily James dressed up in a seventies jumpsuit and gold boots to impersonate a young Donna Sheridan (Meryl Streep). Dancing on top of a canal boat or cycling through the streets, there's a lively rendition of 'When I Kissed the Teacher', backed by euphoric students in gowns and mortar boards.

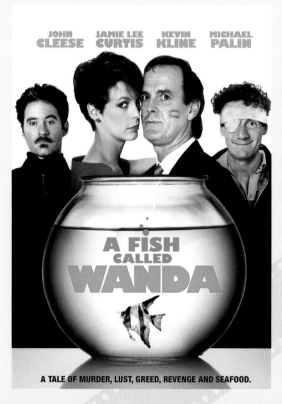

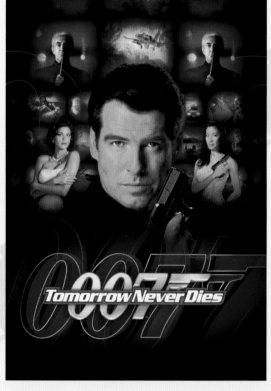

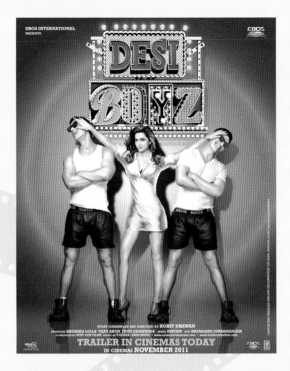

Bollywood and Beyond

In *Desi Boyz* (2011), male escort Jerry Patel meets Economics prof Tanya Sharma (Bollywood star Chitrangda Singh) and pursues her through a variety of Oxford locations singing 'Allah Maaf Kare' ('God forgive me'). Director Rohit Dhawan filmed in Balliol, Queen's, Trinity and other colleges, all populated by synchronised rows of stylised students. Set in an all-male university where love is forbidden, *Mohabbatein* (2000) filmed several scenes in Oxford. It starred Amitabh Bachchan as the strict principal and Shah Rukh Khan as a rebel music teacher – the first of many films they appeared in together.

Rohan (Hrithik Roshan) drives a red sports car into the grand court at Blenheim Palace in the record-grossing *Kabhi Khushi Kabhie Gham* (2001) for the massive song-and-dance number 'Deewana Hai Dekho' ('Look, he's crazy'). The palace represents the college he's just enrolled in, along with Pooja (Kareena Kapoor). In *Salaam-e-Ishq* (2007), a Bollywood version of *Love Actually*, the song 'Tenu Leke' features Radcliffe Square and the outside of the Sheldonian, sandwiched between London locations.

PREVIOUS PAGE LEFT The film poster for *A Fish Called Wanda* (1988) starring Jamie Lee Curtis and John Cleese

PREVIOUS PAGE RIGHT The film poster for *Tomorrow Never Dies* (1997), where Pierce Brosnan, as James Bond, has a close encounter in Oxford

TOP The Bollywood hit *Desi Boyz* (2011) shot dance scenes in a variety of Oxford locations

LEFT The iconic Radcliffe Camera features in lots of films, including Indian romance *Salaam-e-Ishq*

Harry Potter's Oxford

Oxford is a key location for some scenes in the Harry Potter films. The cityscape itself is often reminiscent of the legendary wizarding world: pointed turrets and dim-lit, cobbled lanes, huge old trees and sinister stone figures. Everywhere you look, there are Potter-esque details, from Latin inscriptions to gargoyles, strange-looking necklaces in the Pitt Rivers Museum or medieval astrolabes in the History of Science Museum.

Christ Church

'Welcome to Hogwarts,' says Professor McGonagall (Maggie Smith) in her stern Scottish accent as she greets the nervous first-year students in *Harry Potter and the Philosopher's Stone* (2001). She is standing at the top of Christ Church staircase. The distinctive vaulted ceiling can be seen behind the professor's crooked pointy hat, and behind the students, the high arched windows lighting the stairway.

Christ Church Dining Hall

This was the inspiration for the Great Hall at Hogwarts, was originally completed in 1520 and was, until the 1870s, Oxford's largest hall. Henry VIII's chief carpenter built the hammer-beam ceiling (which, in the films, is often obscured by magical clouds or floating candles) and the walls are hung with portraits that include queens and poets. For the Harry Potter films, an even larger replica hall was built in the studio and it's here that many of the most memorable scenes take place, from the Sorting Hat Ceremony to the Battle of Hogwarts.

Divinity Hall

There's more spectacular vaulting and tall windows in the Bodleian Library's Divinity Hall, which became Hogwarts Infirmary on several occasions. This is where Dumbledore (then Richard Harris) visits Harry towards the end of the first film; it's where Lavender and Hermione visit Ron when he has drunk some poisoned mead in the *Half-Blood Prince* (2009) and where the battered students assemble after the final confrontation at the end of *Deathly Hallows: Part 2* (2011). Divinity Hall, furnished with a giant record player, is also the venue for McGonagall's dance lesson before the Yule Ball in the *Goblet of Fire* (2005).

Hogwarts Library

This was filmed in Duke Humfrey's, an ancient medieval book collection, upstairs from Divinity Hall and accessible on a regular Bodleian mini-tour. Hidden in his invisibility cloak, Harry searches the 'restricted section' with a lantern, looking for information on Nicholas Flamel. The students come back here in *Chamber of Secrets* (2002), looking for the heir of Slytherin, and again to solve the problems of the Triwizard Tournament in *Goblet of Fire*.

PREVIOUS PAGE Duke Humfrey's, the Bodleian's oldest book collection, features in the Harry Potter films as the 'restricted section' of Hogwarts library

ABOVE The British film poster for *Harry Potter and the Philosopher's Stone* (2001), starring clockwise from top centre: Robbie Coltrane, Daniel Radcliffe, Maggie Smith, Alan Rickman, Rupert Grint, Emma Watson and Richard Harris

New College Cloisters

Entered unwillingly into the Triwizard Tournament,
Harry looks angry as he steps down from what are
actually New College Cloisters into the grassy quad.
'Why so tense, Potter?' calls Draco Malfoy, perched
in a holm oak tree above him. As tempers rise, Draco
draws his wand and is promptly turned into a white
ferret by Mad-Eye Moody.

Blenheim Palace

When Harry stumbles into an unhappy memory of
Snape's in the final film, *Deathly Hallows: Part 2*, brief
images in the montage identify a lakeside location at
Blenheim Palace, eight miles northwest of Oxford. A
distinctive tree with a hole in it appears just before
the young James Potter's voice says:
'Come on Moony, Padfoot!'

Pitt Rivers Museum

This wasn't directly used for filming, but there are several artefacts here that clearly influenced designs for the movies, including the shrunken heads that inspired Dre Head in the *Prisoner of Azkaban* (2004). This wonderfully spooky ethnographic museum is redolent of Potter's world: giant hairy spiders, spiral staircases, ritual objects and gloomy gothic arches.

LEFT Christ Church dining hall was the inspiration for the recognisable Great Hall at Hogwarts School of Witchcraft and Wizardry

RIGHT The British film poster for *Harry Potter and the Goblet of Fire* (2005), which filmed one scene in New College cloisters

Around Radcliffe Square

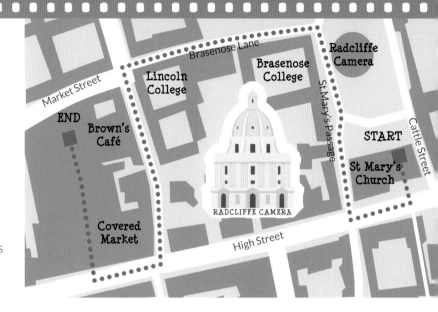

START:
St Mary's Church,
High Street

END:
Covered Market

DISTANCE:
about ⅔ mile (1km)

REFRESHMENTS:
Vaults and Garden Café
under St Mary's; Brown's
Café in Covered Market

Radcliffe
Square,
St Mary's,
Brasenose,
Lincoln and
the Covered
Market

For an overview of Oxford's famous spires, climb the 127 steps up the 13th-century tower of **St Mary's church**, past gargoyles and statues. C.S. Lewis gave the university sermon in this church in 1941 and the view from the top of the tower appears in *Shadowlands* and other films. From the 1987 adaptation of Dorothy L Sayers' *Gaudy Nights*, starring Harriet Walters, to the 2017 remake of *The Mummy* with Tom Cruise, this panorama over Radcliffe Square and neighbouring colleges and streets has featured in many Oxford-based films and TV series.

Exiting right onto the High Street and right again, you pass a doorway with golden fauns carved over it and a **lamppost**, a scene that might have inspired C.S. Lewis' description of Narnia in *The Lion, the Witch and the Wardrobe*. The domed **Radcliffe Camera**, built as a library in the 1730s, is Oxford's most instantly recognisable landmark and has also become a scene-setter in dozens of movies. At the start of *The Golden Compass* (2007), a rippling special effect illuminates the building, illustrating the idea of parallel universes; as if through a

tear between worlds, we travel from one alternative reality (with modern blocks in the background) into Lyra's world, where people's inner selves (or dæmons) accompany them as externalised birds or animals.

On the left of Radcliffe Square, **Brasenose College** has appeared in several episodes of *Inspector Morse* and *Lewis*, becoming Lonsdale College in *Endeavour*, where young Morse stops studying in the 1960s to join the police. In *Young Sherlock Holmes*, Brasenose provided the outside of 'Brompton School' and in *Another Country*, inspired by the biography of spy Guy Burgess, it became another generic public school after Eton refused permission to film there. Stroll round the gardens to see the oval windows through which Guy Bennett passes a note to James Harcourt. When Pierce Brosnan, as James Bond in *Tomorrow Never Dies*, is 'brushing up on a little Danish', a warmly lit aerial shot of Brasenose sets the scene.

Turn left along medieval, pedestrianised Brasenose Lane (a man falls out of a college window here in the 'Trove' episode

NEXT PAGE ABOVE
Film poster for
*Transformers: The
Last Knight*, which
was filmed near
Lincoln College

NEXT PAGE BELOW
The Covered Market
appears in episodes
of *Inspector Morse*
and *Endeavour* on ITV

of *Endeavour*). Turn left again into Turl Street to find **Lincoln College**. Children's writer Dr Seuss and spy novelist John Le Carré were once students here. In the film version of *Brideshead Revisited* (2008), Sebastian Flyte (Ben Whishaw) inhabits the lavish halls of Christ Church while Charles Ryder goes to relatively modest Merton, but different parts of Lincoln were actually used to represent both colleges. Lincoln also featured in *Transformers: The Last Knight* (2017), along with nearby lanes and squares.

Continue along Turl Street, turn right onto the High Street and right again into the **Covered Market.** The *Inspector Morse* episode 'Absolute Conviction' features Brown's café at the back of the market. Endeavour Morse (Shaun Evans) and his mentor DI Thursday (Roger Allam) also pitch up here. The café's timelessly retro interior is a great place to end the walk and they serve full English breakfasts all day.

FEATURED FILMS

The Golden Compass

Young Sherlock Holmes

Another Country

Bodleian Library

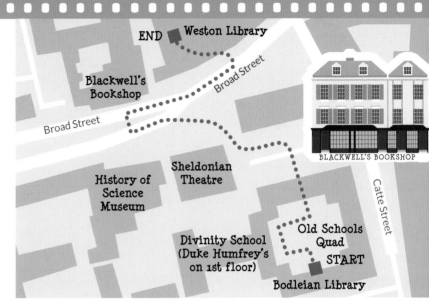

START AND END:
Bodleian Quad

DISTANCE:
about ¼ mile (0.5km)

REFRESHMENTS:
Bodleian café in
Weston Library

Map labels: END • Weston Library • Blackwell's Bookshop • Broad Street • Broad Street • Sheldonian Theatre • History of Science Museum • Divinity School (Duke Humfrey's on 1st floor) • Old Schools Quad • START • Bodleian Library • Catte Street • BLACKWELL'S BOOKSHOP

Bodleian,
Sheldonian,
History of
Science
Museum,
Blackwell's
Bookshop

Start in the huge **Bodleian Old Schools Quad**, surrounded by ancient doorways with stone faces and Latin labels. *X-Men: First Class* (2011), *The Golden Compass* (2007), *The History Boys* and numerous episodes of *Inspector Morse*, *Lewis* and *Endeavour* featured scenes in and around this imposing quadrangle. It's here in the opening scene of *Another Country* (1984) that Guy Bennett (Rupert Everett) catches sight of James Harcourt (Cary Elwes).

Buy a £1 ticket or book a tour and head through the door behind the statue of William Herbert. Keep straight through another door to enter **Divinity Hall**, used to film scenes in Hogwarts Infirmary. Here, under the distinctive high windows of the hall, Madam Pomfrey (Gemma Jones) presides over a small row of hospital beds, and Professor McGonagall (Maggie Smith) tries to teach an embarrassed Ron Weasley to dance in the *Goblet of Fire* (2005). Divinity Hall was also used as a location for *The Madness of King George* (1994): together with neighbouring buildings, the Bodleian's halls doubled as the Houses of Parliament. In a cameo as an MP, author Alan Bennett is just starting to make a speech when the king's coach arrives.

In order to get inside **Duke Humfrey's Library**, on the floor above, you'll need to sign up for a tour (which will also include Divinity Hall). In this atmospheric medieval library, Harry, Ron and Hermione research the philosopher's stone, the basilisk and polyjuice potion. Duke Humfrey's became Hogwarts' Restricted Section, where the books can suddenly start screaming. Real-life students need a special pass to use this library, just as they do in Hogwarts; photography is forbidden, and the books really

were traditionally chained to the shelves. Members of the violent revellers' group in *The Riot Club* (2014) abduct a new member from this library to perform an initiation.

Surrounded by stone heads, the **Sheldonian Theatre** next door, where the university's ceremonies take place, appears in *Shadowlands*. 'Joy wants to see the pageant of learning,' says C.S. Lewis (Anthony Hopkins). The Sheldonian's painted ceiling and curved ranks of seating are also where Charles Xavier gets his doctorate in *X-Men: First Class* and have pretended to be part of Harvard in *Heaven's Gate* (1980). Don't miss climbing up into the cupola for fabulous views of the Bodleian and beyond.

The steps just beyond the Sheldonian lead to the **History of Science Museum**,

packed with interesting stuff, including the box of chemicals Lewis Carroll used to process his photos of Alice, Einstein's blackboard, original mouldy penicillin flasks or Brunel's surveying sextant. Latin dedications in stained glass, dim-lit stairways, ancient clocks and astrolabes all add to the mysterious atmosphere.

Across the road is **Blackwell's,** a venerable family-run bookshop. Inspector Morse interviews Mrs Field here about her husband's murder in 'Who Killed Harry Field' and the White Horse pub next door is a Morse favourite. In the nearby **Weston Library** you can see some of the treasures of the Bodleian collections, including the original story-letters that became Kenneth Grahame's *The Wind in the Willows*. You can buy souvenirs here and have a cup of tea.

BELOW The Bodleian Library, both inside and out, has been a popular film location

17

Malfoy's Tree and More

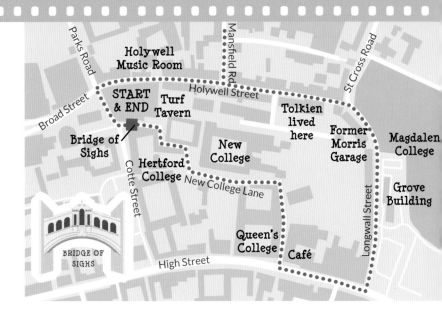

START AND END:
Bridge of Sighs

DISTANCE:
about 1 mile (1.5km)

REFRESHMENTS:
Queens Lane
Coffee House

Bridge
of Sighs,
Hertford,
New College,
Queen's,
Longwall and
Holywell
Streets,
Mansfield
College

NEXT PAGE ABOVE
Draco Malfoy sits
in this tree in New
College cloisters
during one scene in
*Harry Potter and the
Goblet of Fire.*

NEXT PAGE BELOW
Film poster for
X-Men: First Class
(2011), which filmed
scenes in Oxford

In *X-Men: First Class*, after flirting with Oxford student Amy, the young Charles Xavier (James McAvoy) emerges onto Catte Street from a pub with an Eagle sign right next to the iconic **Bridge of Sighs**, part of Hertford College. The Eagle itself does not exist, but the Turf Tavern is hidden nearby. Hertford College was a chief location for the award-winning 1980s TV serial of *Brideshead Revisited*. The fictional Charles Ryder (Jeremy Irons) lives in the actual room once inhabited by author Evelyn Waugh in the 1920s (not open to the public).

Go under the bridge and follow the narrow lane, a sinister setting for Tom Cruise's confrontation with the monster and a horrifying army of rats in *The Mummy* (2017). Through the doorway ahead is **New College**, where actor Hugh Grant was a student. Walk through the front quadrangle, where gargoyles leer from above the chapel and turn left to reach the 14th-century cloisters and the grassy quad in the middle, which feature in *Harry Potter and the Goblet of Fire*. Draco Malfoy looks down from the branches of the distinctive evergreen holm oak tree,

planted in Victorian times. He taunts Harry before Mad-Eye Moody turns him into a ferret.

While you're in New College, don't miss the chapel with Joshua Reynolds' stained glass and wooden faces carved under the seats at the back of the choir stalls. The panelled dining hall, oldest in either Oxford or Cambridge, is also worth a look. Even more ancient are the 12th-century city walls that tower over a colourful herbaceous border.

Continuing past New College into Queen's Lane, emerge onto High Street, where **Queen's College** is on your right (visits by arrangement through the Tourist Office). As Lord Asriel (Daniel Craig) strides through college walkways near the start of *The Golden Compass*, you can see the cupola of Queen's behind him. The college also features in *The Saint* (1997) starring Val Kilmer and the Bollywood hit *Mohabbatein* (2000).

Turn left along the High Street and left again on Longwall Street. The attractive golden sandstone tower inside the back

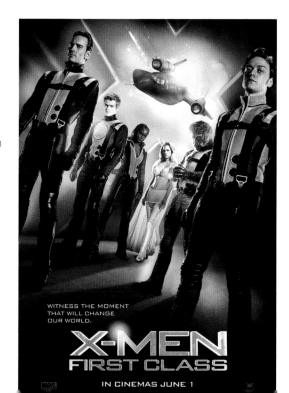

FEATURED FILMS

The Mummy
Tomorrow Never Dies
Harry Potter and
the Goblet of Fire

gate of Magdalen College is part of the Grove Building, built with the proceeds of filming *Shadowlands*. C.S. Lewis was a tutor at Magdalen and much of the film takes place here. Further on, you pass the first Morris garage (brick with big green door) and turn left into Holywell Street. Tolkien lived in the house at number 99 in the early 1950s while at 1 Mansfield Road, on the right, C.S. Lewis spent his first night in Oxford.

Mansfield College, further up Mansfield Road, was a location for *On Chesil Beach* (2017), the story of an awkward 1960s honeymoon that stars Saoirse Ronan with scenes including the CND (Campaign for Nuclear Disarmament) meeting where the protagonists meet. It is based on the novella by Ian McEwan.

Continue along **Holywell Street** to return to Catte Street, past the winter entrance to New College (open 2–4pm), where James Bond (Pierce Brosnan) parks his Aston Martin in *Tomorrow Never Dies*. We see the distinctive silver car and hear Bond's teacher saying (in Danish) that she is pleased with his progress. Cut to

a bedroom scene where Bond is assuring her (still in Danish) that 'practice makes perfect'. Holywell Music Room, towards the end of Holywell Street, is Europe's oldest concert hall; Inspector Morse comes here for both business and pleasure.

19

Museums and Parks

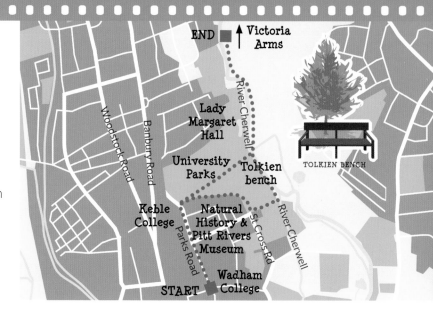

START:
University museums,
Parks Road

END:
Keble College/Victoria
Arms, Marston

DISTANCE:
about 1 mile (1.5km), with
optional 2-mile (3km)
extension at the end

REFRESHMENTS:
Museum café;
Victoria Arms

END ⬛ ↑ Victoria
Arms

River Cherwell

Lady
Margaret
Hall

Woodstock Road

Banbury Road

University
Parks

Tolkien
bench

TOLKIEN BENCH

Keble
College

Natural
History &
Pitt Rivers
Museum

St Cross Rd

River Cherwell

Parks Road

Wadham
College

START

**University
museums and
parks, Keble
College, River
Cherwell**

The University Museums have inspired several Oxford stories as well as film and TV designs. As you walk through the **Museum of Natural History**, with its dried puffer fish and dinosaur bones, don't miss the case full of animals from Lewis Carroll's books: hedgehogs and flamingos, a white rabbit and a (reconstructed) dodo. Carroll worked creatures from the museum's collections into his Alice stories.

Go through the arch at the back of the hall into the spooky dimness of the **Pitt Rivers Museum**. This fabulous collection of ethnographic treasures includes shrunken heads, which were copied for the dreadlocked head, voiced by Lenny Henry, at the front of the ghostly Knight Bus in *Harry Potter and the Prisoner of Azkaban* (2004). J.K. Rowling may have based the contents of some of the wizarding shops in Diagon Alley on the mysterious objects in this magical museum.

Philip Pullman was inspired by these collections too, conjuring up the idea of an alethiometer, a mysterious truth-telling device. There are similar instruments with arcane symbols on them as well as skulls

with holes in – and tools for trepanning; in *Northern Lights* (the novel *The Golden Compass* was based on), the Tartar people do this to let 'dust' into their brains. You can also see arctic coats very similar to some of the movie's costumes.

In the *Inspector Morse* episode 'Daughters of Cain', a knife stolen from the museum is used as a murder weapon. The knife is a real exhibit – you can find it at the bottom of the introductory case, to the left inside the entrance. For more weaponry, head up to the second floor, full of bloodthirsty spiked maces and samurai suits.

Cross the road to **Keble College.** In an episode of *Endeavour* called 'Home' (2013), a snow-covered Keble becomes 'Baidley College', while young Morse is investigating the murder of an Oxford don. If you visit the college, don't miss a glimpse of its famously long dining hall or Holman Hunt's *Light of the World* in the chapel. **Wadham College**, on the same road, appeared in three episodes of *Inspector Morse* and is the alma mater of Rosamund Pike (*Pride and Prejudice*, *Gone Girl*) and Felicity Jones (*Theory of Everything*, *Rogue One*).

NEXT PAGE ABOVE
Film poster for
*Harry Potter and the
Prisoner of Azkaban*
(2004)

NEXT PAGE BELOW
Oxford University's
Pitt Rivers Museum
has inspired authors
and film designers

Opposite Keble is a gate into the **University Parks**. Walk straight ahead following the right-hand edge of the park until you see the river ahead and turn left along it. From a Japanese Pagoda tree to Corsican pines and wild cherries, there's a rich variety of foliage here. In 1992, a hundred years after Tolkien's birth, two trees were planted here with a **memorial bench** nearby. The trees represent the silver and gold trees of Valinor in Tolkien's mythology. Reaching the High Bridge, a footbridge arching over the river, turn left again along the South Walk to return to Parks Road near Keble.

For a longer walk, you could cross the bridge and walk along the far side of the river, passing the grounds of **Lady Margaret Hall** (LMH) across the water. Students at LMH include Nobel-prize winner Malala Yousafzai, and Emma Watson, who played Hermione Granger in the Harry Potter films, is a visiting fellow. Crossing under the Marston Ferry Road, you can continue all the way to the riverside **Victoria Arms** near Marston (open from 12 noon), a repeated location in ITV's *Inspector Morse*, *Lewis* and *Endeavour*. Morse has a final drink here in 'The Remorseful Day' (2000), his last episode.

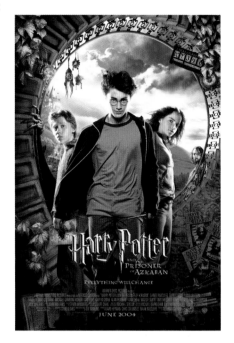

FEATURED
FILMS

Harry Potter and the
Prisoner of Azkaban

Inspector Morse

Endeavour

Lyra's Playground

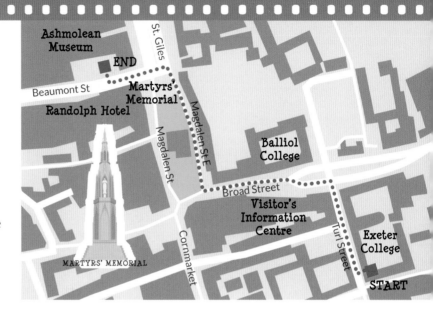

START:
Exeter College

END:
Ashmolean Museum

DISTANCE:
about ²/₃ mile (1km)

REFRESHMENTS:
Ashmolean cafés, Morse
Bar in Randolph Hotel

Exeter College,
Broad Street,
Beaumont
Street,
Ashmolean
Museum

Start at **Exeter College** on Turl Street (open free most afternoons). Philip Pullman's old college is the model for Jordan in *Northern Lights*, which became the film *The Golden Compass* (2007). Lyra prevents her uncle Lord Asriel from being poisoned after hiding in a cupboard here. Pullman recalls crawling along the gutters above Exeter just as Lyra, in his book, scales the 'irregular Alps of the College roofs'. Exeter's roof-scape was recreated in a studio for the film. Don't miss the great view of the Radcliffe Camera from the raised garden behind the college. J.R.R. Tolkien, actor Richard Burton and writer Alan Bennett were all students here at various times and J.K. Rowling is an honorary fellow.

Exeter's **Chapel,** with its tall stained-glass windows, appears in Marvel's *Doctor Strange* (2016), starring Benedict Cumberbatch. Staring fiendishly out of three hours' worth of extraordinary eye make-up, Danish actor Mads Mikkelsen, as rebel mystic Kaecilius, practises dark arts here. In the last episode of *Inspector Morse*, 'The Remorseful Day', the detective had his fatal heart attack in Exeter's gardens as Fauré's *Requiem* played from the nearby chapel.

ABOVE Poster for *The Golden Compass* (2007), which was set and filmed partly in Oxford

BELOW Exeter College was the model for Jordan College in *The Golden Compass*

Turn right out of Exeter and left on Broad Street to find the **Oxford Visitor Information Centre** where you can buy maps and souvenirs, from booklets about the city's literary haunts to your very own wand and furry Hedwig. You can also book Potter and Alice, Tolkien or Pullman-themed guided tours here.

Members of *The Riot Club* ride down **Broad Street** at midnight, swigging champagne from the bottle in an open-top Aston Martin.

After one of them vomits over the plush interior, they abandon the car with a throwaway comment that 'the ashtray was full anyway'. The entrance on the far side of Broad Street leads into **Balliol**, a location for both *Inspector Morse* and *Lewis*. At the end of Broad Street, turn right to the Martyrs' Memorial; it appears, along with nearby sights, in 'The Wolvercote Tongue' episode of *Inspector Morse*.

Cross the wide road left, past the memorial, to the Victorian gothic **Randolph Hotel.** This city institution has renamed one cosy watering hole 'the Morse Bar' as a tribute to the hotel's many appearances in the ITV series; there are photos over the fireplace and even a calvados and champagne cocktail named after the grumpy detective, although Morse might have preferred a decent pint of bitter. In *Shadowlands*, C.S. Lewis (Anthony Hopkins) first meets Joy Gresham (Debra Winger) here, in what was then the Fellows bar; you can see the neo-classical Ashmolean through the windows behind (the couple actually met in the Eastgate Hotel on the High Street).

The **Ashmolean Museum** over the road is open daily and packed with treasures from around the world and throughout the millennia; from mummy case portraits to pre-Raphaelite paintings. Watch out for the case of gold Posy rings that look very like Tolkien's 'one ring', inscribed inside with quotes in French or Latin.

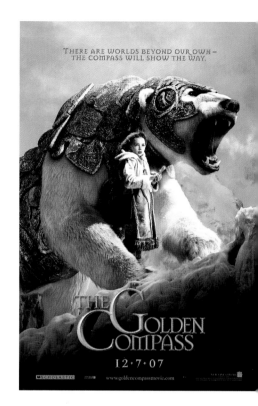

THERE ARE WORLDS BEYOND OUR OWN – THE COMPASS WILL SHOW THE WAY.

THE GOLDEN COMPASS

12·7·07

www.goldencompassmovie.com

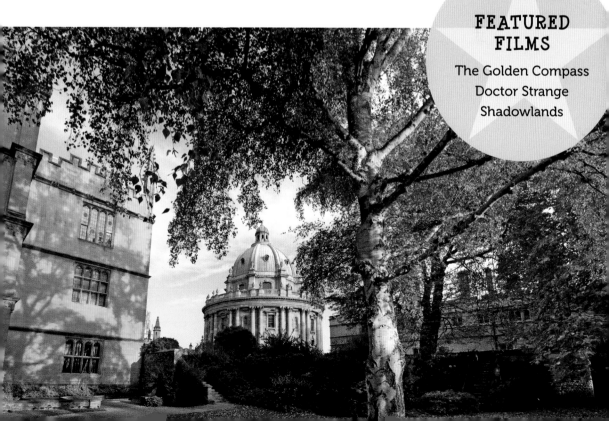

FEATURED FILMS

The Golden Compass
Doctor Strange
Shadowlands

Heart of Town

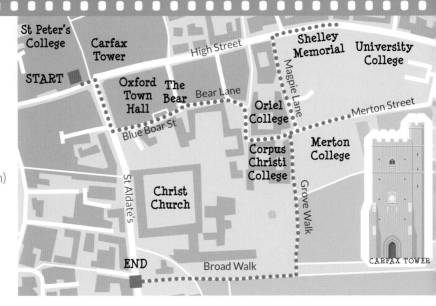

St Peter's College · Carfax Tower · High Street · Shelley Memorial · University College

START · Oxford Town Hall · The Bear · Bear Lane · Oriel College · Magpie Lane · Merton Street

Blue Boar St · Corpus Christi College · Merton College · Grove Walk

St Aldate's · Christ Church · Broad Walk · CARFAX TOWER

END

START:
Carfax Tower

END:
St Aldate's

DISTANCE:
about 1½ miles (2.5km)

REFRESHMENTS:
Bear Inn

Carfax,
St Aldate's,
Oriel Square,
Merton Street,
Christ Church
Meadows

NEXT PAGE ABOVE
Merton Street is a
popular location for
historical films and
costume dramas

NEXT PAGE BELOW
Film poster for
Testament of Youth
(2014), which shot
some scenes on
Merton Street

Start at Carfax crossroads, Oxford's ancient heart. You can get another bird's eye view of the city and along the busy High Street by climbing the narrow spiral staircase of 12th-century **Carfax Tower.** Ken Loach, known for his socially engaged films from *Kes* in the 1960s to *I, Daniel Blake* (2016), studied Law at St Peter's College in nearby New Inn Hall Street.

Walk down St Aldate's. The Victorian interior of **Oxford Town Hall** (tours only, £4.50) doubled as the inside of the Old Bailey in *A Fish Called Wanda* (1988). It also became the 'Ethical Hall', where Leonard Bast and the Schlegel sisters (Emma Thompson and Helena Bonham-Carter) hear a lecture and Helen picks up the wrong umbrella in *Howards End* (1992). Inside the town hall, you'll also find the Oxford Museum.

Turn left down Blue Boar Street to reach the **Bear Inn** (open from 11am). This pub, one of the city's oldest, has a collection of nearly 5000 snipped-off ties. In Colin Dexter's novel *Death is Now my Neighbour*, Inspector Morse asks the landlord for help identifying a tie, which had become

a crucial clue. Keep on into Bear Lane to reach several lovely colleges.

Hugh Grant made his screen debut at **Oriel College** in a student film called *Privileged* (1982). Oriel, which also makes several appearances in *Inspector Morse* and *Lewis*, is the college where Nick (Rob Lowe) is supposed to be studying in *Oxford Blues* (1984) and features in the rowing film *True Blue* (1996) with Dominic West, Tom Hollander and others. The street outside was one of several Oxford locations for *Quills* (2000), a film about the Marquis de Sade, starring Geoffrey Rush and Kate Winslet.

Nearby, with gold pelicans topping its drainpipes and a distinctive column in the courtyard, **Corpus Christi** is the college Dakin (Dominic Cooper) visits in *The History Boys* (2006), finding out that Irwin was never a student there. The montage of Oxford shots at the start of the TV adaptation of Dorothy L Sayers' *Gaudy Nights* (1987) follows the sound of organ music into Corpus chapel. The story is set in a fictional all-female college called Shrewsbury, based on Sayers' old college, Somerville.

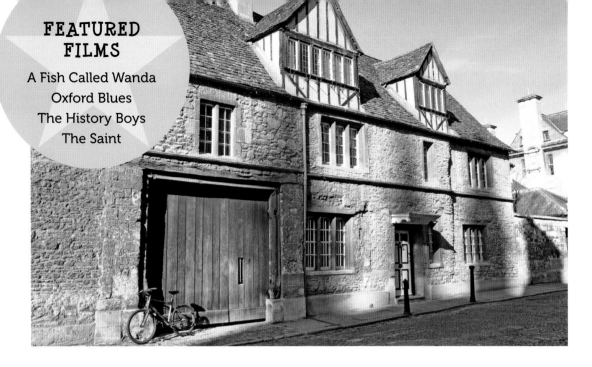

FEATURED FILMS

A Fish Called Wanda
Oxford Blues
The History Boys
The Saint

FROM THE PRODUCER OF THE BOY IN THE STRIPED PYJAMAS

★ ★ ★ ★
"STUNNINGLY GOOD...
DESPERATELY MOVING"
David Sexton, Evening Standard

★ ★ ★ ★
"HEARTFELT... STIRRING...
AND DEEPLY SATISFYING"
Wendy Ide, The Times

★ ★ ★ ★
"A POWERFUL... MOVING...
HEARTBREAKER"
Screen International

★ ★ ★ ★
"VIKANDER GIVES A
GLORIOUS PERFORMANCE"
Tim Robey, Telegraph

Divided by War.   *United by Love.*

Alicia *Kit* *Emily* *Hayley* *Colin* *Dominic* *Miranda*
VIKANDER HARINGTON WATSON ATWELL MORGAN and WEST and RICHARDSON

TESTAMENT *of* YOUTH

BASED ON THE POWERFUL BEST-SELLING MEMOIR BY VERA BRITTAIN

IN CINEMAS JANUARY 16

Next door is **Merton College**. *Testament of Youth* (2014), based on Vera Brittain's memoir with Alicia Vikander playing Brittain, was partly filmed in Merton Street, and Merton College again stood in for Somerville. The beautiful 'Mob Quad' in Merton is Oxford's oldest quadrangle; J.R.R. Tolkien, professor here from 1945 to 1959, had rooms in Fellows Quad, overlooking Christ Church Meadow and later lived on Merton Street.

To visit one more college in the area, cross Merton Street into Magpie Lane, which appears in *Iris* (2001). It emerges on the High Street near **University College**. Turn right to reach it and right again, inside the gates, to see the statue of naked, dead Shelley, carved from white marble, where Simon Templar tries to seduce Oxford don Emma Russell in *The Saint* (1997) as she admires the memorial and 'the way the light holds him in silence.'

Return to Merton and keep straight down Grove Walk and on through the gate beyond into the meadow. The grass to your left features in *Accident* (1967) as the site of an emotionally charged cricket match. Turn right along Broad Walk, past Christ Church, to reach St Aldate's again.

Welcome to Hogwarts

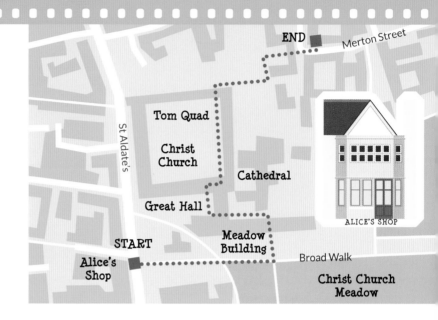

START:
St Aldate's

END:
Oriel Square

DISTANCE:
about 1/4 mile (0.5km)

REFRESHMENTS:
St Aldate's

Christ Church
College,
Alice's Shop

NEXT PAGE LEFT The grand staircase in Christ Church became the entrance to Hogwarts in *Harry Potter and the Philosopher's Stone*

NEXT PAGE RIGHT Alice's Shop inspired an illustration in *Alice Through the Looking-Glass* and now sells souvenirs

Both a college and a cathedral, **Christ Church** is one of the most famous and beautiful Oxford institutions. Scenes from *Harry Potter* and *The Golden Compass* were filmed in the cloisters, staircase and hall. From Christ Church meadows, off St Aldate's, enter through the Victorian Meadow Building and follow the signs inside to reach the **Hall Staircase**, with its spectacular vaulted ceiling.

As the first years shuffle into the Hogwarts in *Harry Potter and the Philosopher's Stone*, we see this staircase first from behind the imposing silhouette of Professor McGonagall (Maggie Smith), standing at the top of the stairs to greet the new students. When Neville Longbottom retrieves his pet toad Trevor from the flagged floor, there is a wonderful shot, from his low-level perspective, of McGonagall's disapproving face towering over him with the fan ceiling radiating above her pointed hat. Mrs Coulter collects Lyra from the sunlit foot of the same staircase in *The Golden Compass*.

Passing through the door at the top of the stairs into the **Great Hall** brings another

scene from the Harry Potter movies instantly to life. The largest pre-Victorian dining hall of any Oxbridge college, Christ Church hall has a portrait of college founder Henry VIII presiding at the far end. Inspired by Christ Church, Hogwarts Hall was created in a studio for the many dining scenes in Harry Potter. Charles Dodgson, aka Lewis Carroll, author of the Alice books, studied at Christ Church in the early 1850s and stayed on as a Maths lecturer. His portrait hangs in the Great Hall, and you can see Alice and the Dodo in one of the stained-glass windows there. Even the hall's fire irons, shaped like long-necked women, must have lodged in Carroll's imagination.

Imposing **Tom Quad** has featured in several films, including in *The Golden Compass*, where a giant gold and red zeppelin is hovering in front of the main gateway's Tom Tower. While you're here, do visit the ancient **cathedral.** The choir here provided the music for the *Vicar of Dibley* (with Dawn French), which was set in Oxfordshire and filmed in nearby Buckinghamshire. Edward Burne-Jones, a late pre-Raphaelite artist, designed some of the cathedral's stained-glass windows. In the Chapel of Remembrance, Burne-Jones has given the face of Edith Liddell (sister of Alice, who inspired the Alice books) to the saint in the central window. Don't miss the **cloister** next door. It's here (with a few added flaming torches) that Harry learns about the magical game of Quidditch, and Hermione shows him a trophy with his father's name on it.

Not only did Christ Church provide the setting for numerous films, but it also nurtured several literary and cinematic talents (as well as thirteen UK prime ministers). The poet W.H. Auden studied here, and you can see a memorial to him on the cathedral floor. Film lovers may remember Matthew (John Hannah) in *Four Weddings and a Funeral* reading W.H. Auden's poem 'Funeral Blues' after the death of his lover, Gareth (Simon Callow). Indeed, Four Weddings writer Richard Curtis, whose romcom scripts have become major Hollywood hits, was also a student here. While at Oxford, Curtis met Rowan Atkinson (*Mr Bean*, *Blackadder*), who studied at Queen's. Harry Lloyd (Viserys Targaryen in *Games of Thrones*) is another former Christ Church student.

Across St Aldate's from the college is the painted **Alice's Shop**: this little medieval building inspired the original illustration of the Old Sheep Shop in *Alice Through the Looking-Glass*. There are also plenty of pubs and cafés nearby.

FEATURED FILMS

Harry Potter
The Golden Compass
Alice in Wonderland

Gateway to Narnia

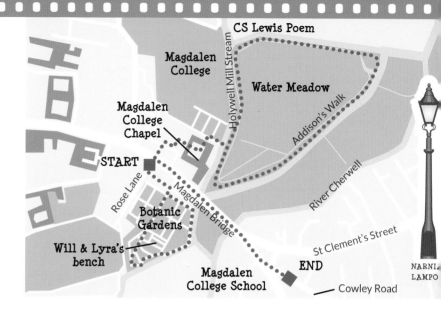

START:
Rose Lane

END:
Cowley Road

DISTANCE:
about 2 miles (3km)

REFRESHMENTS:
Magdalen Old Kitchen
Bar, Cowley Road

Map labels: CS Lewis Poem · Magdalen College · Water Meadow · Holywell Mill Stream · Addison's Walk · Magdalen College Chapel · START · Rose Lane · Magdalen Bridge · River Cherwell · Botanic Gardens · Will & Lyra's bench · Magdalen College School · END · St Clement's Street · Cowley Road · NARNIA LAMPO

University
of Oxford
Botanic
Garden and
Magdalen
College

A maze of roses off Oxford's High Street leads to the **Botanic Garden**, one of the world's most diverse but compact plant collections. An old pine tree here helped inspire Tolkien's 'Ents', the sentient trees in *The Lord of the Rings* (sadly it was cut down in 2014 after two of its branches fell off). Will and Lyra promise to meet here in Philip Pullman's *The Amber Spyglass* on a bench that exists in both their parallel worlds and in real life: it's by a pond at the far end of the garden.

You can see the Lily House in the background of the original illustration for the queen's croquet lawn in Lewis Carroll's *Alice's Adventures in Wonderland*, and you'll find a grinning Cheshire cat carved into a tree, just beyond the fountain. The greenhouses recall Harry Potter's Herbology classes – you can imagine Professor Sprout giving instructions as her students transplant screeching mandrakes.

Across the road, **Magdalen College** is a popular film location, appearing in at least five episodes of *Inspector Morse* and *Lewis*; its former students include Oscar

Wilde and Andrew Lloyd Webber. In *The History Boys*, Posner and Akhtar discuss their interviews here. Narnia author C.S. Lewis taught here and the college appears throughout *Shadowlands* (1993), the film about his life. Stone animals carved onto the nearby cloisters may well have inspired the White Witch's statues in *The Lion, the Witch and the Wardrobe*.

Shadowlands opens in Magdalen's medieval **chapel**, with the camera panning up and down the rows of carved saints behind the altar, and goes on to a formal dinner in Magdalen's panelled hall. Later Lewis (Anthony Hopkins) gives Joy Gresham (Debra Winger) a tour of the college, walking through the cloisters and pointing out the Palladian 'New' Building ('1733,' he tells her), where he lived on staircase 3.

The bridge over **Holywell Mill Stream** through an iron gate near the New Building is where Charles Ryder (Matthew Goode) first catches sight of Sebastian Flyte (Ben Whishaw) in the 2008 film of *Brideshead Revisited*, and where Margaret Schlegel (Emma

NEXT PAGE ABOVE
Film poster for *The Chronicles of Narnia: The Lion, the Witch and the Wardrobe* (2005). C.S. Lewis, author of the Narnia books, taught at Magdalen College

NEXT PAGE BELOW
Oxford's Botanic Garden has inspired several authors

Thompson) meets her brother in *Howards End* (1992). It's also the location for a fateful punting trip in *Accident* (1967).

Cross the bridge and turn right to take a stroll around beautiful **Addison's Walk** and watch the punts poling under Magdalen Bridge. The water meadows in the centre of the walkway are covered with rare snake's head fritillaries in spring and are home to the college deer herd from July to December. C.S. Lewis walked here with Tolkien and one late night conversation in 1931 helped restore Lewis's battered belief in God. A poem on the wall, near a view of the mill, reflects the writer's faith that 'This year the summer will come true.' This rekindled faith is evident throughout *The Chronicles of Narnia*.

Returning to the High Street, turn left over **Magdalen Bridge**, where a body is found floating in one episode of *Endeavour*. In *Shadowlands*, C.S. Lewis goes to the traditional May Morning celebration with his wife, and they hear the choristers singing *Hymnus Eucharisticus* from the top of the tower; revellers jump into the water as the sun rises through riverside mists. Continuing along the busy High Street, you reach a roundabout known as the Plain. Magdalen College School is on the right, where director Sam Mendes (*American Beauty*, *Skyfall*) was a student. Cowley Road, straight on beyond the roundabout, has lots of great restaurants.

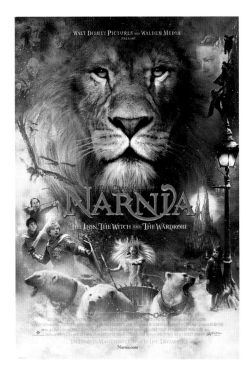

FEATURED FILMS

Shadowlands

Brideshead Revisited

Howards End

An Oxford Pub Crawl

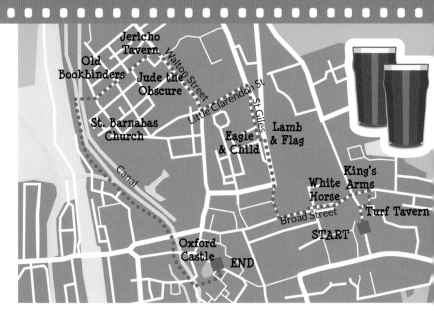

START:
Radcliffe Camera

END:
Oxford Castle

DISTANCE:
about 3 miles (5km)

REFRESHMENTS:
throughout

Turf Tavern,
White Horse,
Eagle and
Child, Jericho
Tavern, Canal,
Oxford Prison

FEATURED FILMS

X-Men: First Class
Endeavour

Inspector Morse

Wilde

102 Dalmatians

Follow in the footsteps of Inspectors Morse and Lewis or of real-life writers like J.R.R. Tolkien, C.S. Lewis and others as you drink your way across town. Walk under the Bridge of Sighs, as Charles Xavier (James McAvoy) does in *X-Men: First Class*, and turn immediately down an alleyway to find the **Turf Tavern** (open from 11am), a Morse favourite. Emerging, via another alley, onto Holywell Street, turn left to find the **King's Arms**, (opens 10.30am) a location for *Inspector Morse* in 'Deadly Slumber' and 'The Secret of Bay 5B'.

Just a few steps away, along Broad Street, is the **White Horse**, which appears in at least six episodes of *Inspector Morse* (as it boasts on a board outside), as well as *Lewis* and *Endeavour*, and features in *The Oxford Murders* (2008), starring Elijah Wood and John Hurt. Walk to the end of Broad Street and turn right along Magdalen Street and keep going to the Lamb and Flag; the young Morse had drinks in this pub with a beautiful opera singer in the pilot episode of *Endeavour*.

Cross wide St Giles to the venerable **Eagle and Child** (open from 11am) where the Inklings, a literary discussion group that included Tolkien and C.S. Lewis, used to meet in the 'Rabbit Room'. The room is still there and lined with memorabilia. Continue to walk up St Giles, turn left along Little Clarendon Street and right into Walton Street (as Lyra does in *Lyra's Oxford*) to the **Jude the Obscure** pub.

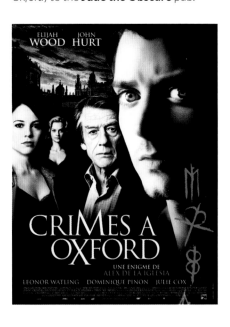

Thomas Hardy's fictional Christminster was based on Oxford University, but the 1996 film *Jude*, starring Christopher Eccleston and Kate Winslet, was filmed mostly in Durham and Edinburgh.

Turn left just before the **Jericho Tavern** where Morse drops in for a beer or two in 'The Silent World of Nicholas Quinn' to drown his disappointment that the cinema next door is unexpectedly showing *101 Dalmatians* rather than *Last Tango in Paris*. Continue along Jericho Street and into Victor Street to the **Old Bookbinders,** which, together with neighbouring Combe Road, featured in the first ever episode of *Inspector Morse*, 'The Dead of Jericho'. Nearby St Barnabas Church appears as St Silas in Thomas Hardy's *Jude the Obscure*.

Jericho was Oxford's first industrial suburb, home of ironwork and bookbinding. Philip Pullman wove this heritage and the 'little brick terraced houses in the narrow lanes' of Jericho into his parallel version of Oxford in the novel that became *The Golden Compass* (2007). In *Northern Lights* and in *Lyra's Oxford*, Pullman has the boat-dwelling Gyptians moor up in

Jericho. In real life, the author was involved in the fight to save the local boatyard from inappropriate development.

Turn right along Canal Street and, where the road bends right, turn left instead and cross the **canal**, a regular *Inspector Morse* location. Turn left beside the canal with water on both sides, past views of the boatyard and St Barnabas. Keep straight over a footbridge and, reaching busy Hythe Bridge Street, cross the bridge and the road to continue along the canal in the same direction.

After one more road, turn left around an ancient tower to find **Oxford Castle**, the historical site of Oxford Prison. Beautiful con artist Wanda Gershwitz (Jamie Lee Curtis) approaches George's barrister, Archie Leach (John Cleese) outside the old prison in *A Fish Called Wanda*. The prison also doubled as Reading Gaol, where Oscar Wilde (Stephen Fry) is locked up at the end of *Wilde* (1997). And a supposedly reformed Cruella de Vil (Glenn Close) walks out of Oxford Prison at the start of *102 Dalmatians* (2000). The prison is now a fancy hotel.

PREVIOUS PAGE Italian film poster for *The Oxford Murders* (2008), starring Elijah Wood and John Hurt

ABOVE LEFT Inspector Morse (John Thaw) and Sergeant Lewis (Kevin Whately) have drunk on-screen pints in numerous Oxford pubs...

ABOVE RIGHT ...including the popular White Horse pub on Broad Street

Messing About on the River

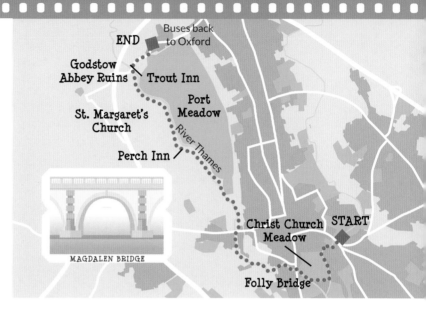

START:
Magdalen Bridge

END:
Wolvercote Village

DISTANCE:
about 5 miles (8km)

REFRESHMENTS:
Trout Inn

MAGDALEN BRIDGE

Christ Church
Meadow,
Folly Bridge,
Port Meadow,
Godstow

From *Wind in the Willows* to the *Book of Dust* and from *Inspector Morse* to *Mamma Mia*, Thames-side scenes appear frequently on screens and in storybooks. You can discover them on this beautiful walk: a stroll through waterside meadows and on along the way-marked Thames Path.

Opposite Magdalen College, walk along Rose Lane and continue, through a gate, along the fence of the University of Oxford Botanic Garden. Keep straight, with the River Cherwell on your left, along a lovely winding path, past idyllic **Christ Church Meadow**. The first scenes of *The Golden Compass* (2007) take place here, after the opening narration. Ma Costa, standing under these trees with her hawk dæmon on her shoulder, calls to Roger before the boat-dwelling Gyptian children and the kids from the colleges chase each other through the fields, with the spires and turrets of Oxford in the background. This is the same view that introduces scenes in *Shadowlands* (1993).

Keeping the water on your left, walk along the bank of the Thames. With

NEXT PAGE Punts near Magdalen Bridge at the start of a waterside adventure along the River Cherwell and River Thames

Folly Bridge ahead, follow the path right and turn left over a little footbridge, through a gate, and round the Head of the River pub. On a legendary golden mid-Victorian afternoon, Oxford Maths professor and cleric Charles Dodgson (aka Lewis Carroll) rowed Alice Liddell and her sisters along the Thames from here and entertained them with surreal adventure stories. *Alice in Wonderland* was published in 1865 and has since inspired dozens of films, most recently Tim Burton's 2010 version starring Johnny Depp.

Turn left over Folly Bridge and then right along the Thames Path, recreating Lewis Carroll's nineteenth-century journey. Simply keep the water on your right until you reach the Botley Road. Cross the road and continue, with the Thames now on your left. Keep going, (with water soon on both sides), following the path left over a footbridge with lovely views across Port Meadow. A short path leads left here to **The Perch**, a seventeenth-century pub that Lewis and Hathaway often visit. The Perch and The Trout Inn were also favourite pubs for the Inklings,

FEATURED FILMS

The Golden Compass
Alice in Wonderland
Mamma Mia!
Here We Go Again

the writers' group that included J.R.R. Tolkien and C.S. Lewis.

Lewis Carroll fans can follow the little lane beyond the pub to reach the simple Norman church of **St Margaret at Binsey**. The ancient 'treacle well' in the churchyard inspired part of *Alice in Wonderland*. Return to the river and continue along it to reach the ruins of **Godstow Abbey,** which features in Philip Pullman's 2017 novel *La Belle Sauvage*, the first part of his *Book of Dust* trilogy. Pullman's Malcolm Polstead lives and works with his parents at the nearby Trout Inn, helps the nuns in the Abbey to look after baby Lyra, and spends much of the book on the water.

Turning right over the nearby bridge, you reach **The Trout Inn**, another venerable seventeenth-century riverside pub and favourite with Inspector Morse. *Mamma Mia!* prequel/sequel *Here We Go Again* filmed scenes nearby, after capturing younger versions of the famous cast cycling through the centre of Oxford. Actors dressed in student gowns dance to more of Abba's greatest hits while young Donna (Lily James) and friends jump off the roof of a canal boat. Oxford professor Dr Emma Russell also visits the pub in *The Saint* (1997). Keep going along the road into Wolvercote village, passing two more pubs. Reaching the bus stop in Home Close on your left, catch one of the frequent buses back to the centre of Oxford.

Beautiful Blenheim

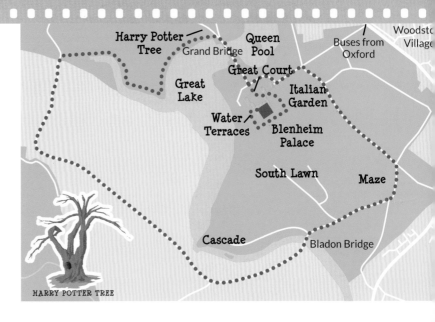

START AND END:
Blenheim Palace

DISTANCE:
about 5 miles (8km)
with shorter options

REFRESHMENTS:
Water Terrace café

Harry Potter Tree · Grand Bridge · Queen Pool · Buses from Oxford · Woodstock Village · Great Court · Great Lake · Italian Garden · Water Terraces · Blenheim Palace · South Lawn · Maze · Cascade · Bladon Bridge

HARRY POTTER TREE

Gardens,
Palladian
architecture,
state rooms,
rolling
parkland,
lakes

Film lovers can easily spend a whole day at Blenheim: the baroque palace, formal gardens and magical landscaped park are beautiful, historical and packed with recognisable scenes from dozens of well-known films, including instalments of James Bond and Harry Potter, *The Young Victoria* (2009) and many more.

Exterior shots of Elsinore castle for Kenneth Branagh's *Hamlet* (1996) are Blenheim Palace; the interiors were filmed in Shepperton Studios, but suggest some influence from Blenheim's décor. In *The Avengers* (1998), with Ralph Fiennes and Uma Thurman, Blenheim became 'Hallucinogen Hall', the huge estate belonging to evil scientist August de Wynter (Sean Connery). King William makes Orlando (Tilda Swinton) an ambassador here in *Orlando* (1992).

NEXT PAGE TOP Film poster for *Spectre* (2015), starring Daniel Craig as the world famous 007 agent

RIGHT The Water Terraces at Blenheim were a location for *The Libertine* (2004), starring Johnny Depp

The imposing columns and pediments of the **Great Court** also became the Italian Palazzo Cadenza, a criminal HQ in *Spectre* (2015), the entrance to a lavish black-tie event in *Mission: Impossible – Rogue Nation* (2015), a Lilliputian backdrop for Jack Black in *Gulliver's Travels* (2010) and a substitute for Versailles in *A Little Chaos* (2014). In *Transformers: The Last Knight* (2017), Nazi flags hung on either side of the palace entrance – slightly ironic for Winston Churchill's old home!

Heading inside the palace, follow the red-carpet walkway through the **Great Hall** to the **Green Writing Room**, where Ethan Hunt (Tom Cruise) meets the Prime Minister in *Rogue Nation*. Next door, the **Saloon** became a decadent backdrop for Johnny Depp in *The Libertine* (2004) and the **First State Room** was the king's bedchamber in the first scene of *A Little Chaos* with Alan Rickman and Kate Winslet. Keep going to find the spectacular **Long Library**, which hosted a charity auction in *Rogue Nation*. Belgian King Leopold plans his royal matchmaking here in *The Young Victoria*.

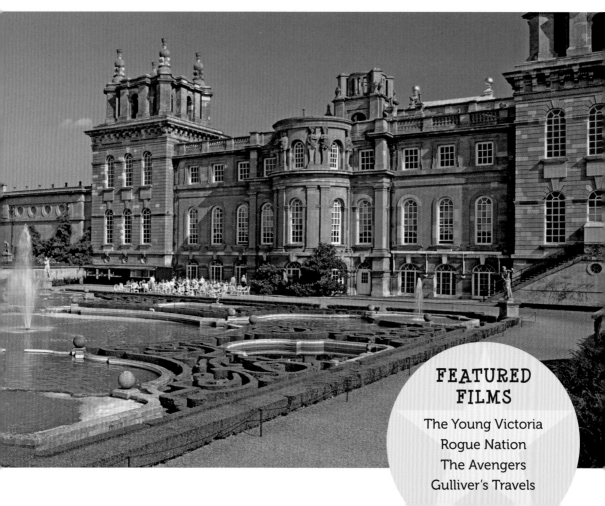

FEATURED FILMS

The Young Victoria
Rogue Nation
The Avengers
Gulliver's Travels

TOP This hollow tree beside the Great Lake makes a fleeting appearance in the fifth Harry Potter film

ABOVE Poster for *Harry Potter and the Order of the Phoenix* (2007)

Stepping out into the gardens, walk through the west colonnade, recognisable from several films, and into the lovely **Water Terraces**, another location for Johnny Depp's *Libertine*. Stanley Kubrick's *Barry Lyndon* strolls, with the countess, through this garden, one of the 1975 film's dizzying number of locations. Turning left onto the South Lawn, another *Gulliver* location, you can admire more views of the palace. The dancers end on the grass here after the marathon montage that accompanies the song 'Deewana Hai Dekho' in Bollywood mega-hit *Kabhi Khushi Kabhie Gham* (2001). Nearby, the **Italian Garden** appeared in *The BFG* (2016) starring Mark Rylance.

In front of the palace, a road leads over the **Grand Bridge** towards the distant Column of Victory. Cinderella (Lily James) rides over this bridge in her coach on the way to the ball in Kenneth Branagh's 2015 film. Looking left from the bridge at the shore of the Great Lake,

keen-eyed Harry Potter fans may recognise a striking **tree with a huge hole** in it. This area was used as the location for a scene in *Order of the Phoenix* when Harry suddenly finds himself inside Snape's memories and sees his own father bullying young Severus. On the far side of the bridge, follow the path left and left again through a wooden gate to take a closer look at the remarkable tree.

You can now head back towards the palace or take a four-mile stroll through the park. For the longer route, walk along the lakeside path with the water on your left, passing a well. When the path finally reaches one end of the lake, continue through a wooden gate and left onto a tarmac lane. Follow this lane for three miles through woods and parkland, passing a back gate into the estate which features in the 'Way through the Woods' episode of *Inspector Morse*.

Cross the elegant **Bladon Bridge** (another *Cinderella* location) and keep on along the lane ahead to reach the Pleasure Gardens. This trove of delights includes a butterfly house and a model of the neighbouring town of Woodstock. **The Marlborough Maze** appears in another episode of *Inspector Morse*. If you've had enough walking by now, a miniature train can take you back to the palace from here.

TOP Film poster for *Cinderella* (2015), starring Lily James, which used several Blenheim locations for its fairy tale settings

BOTTOM The spectacular parkland and palace have attracted dozens of filmmakers

Discover Downton

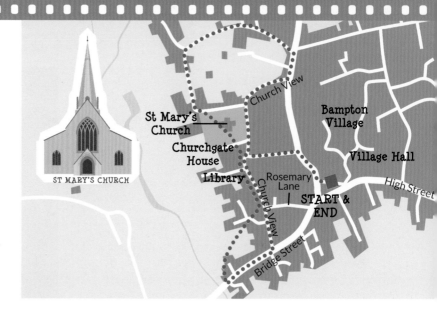

START AND END:
Bampton's Market Square

DISTANCE:
1 mile (1.5km) around Bampton and ¼ mile (0.5km) around Cogges

REFRESHMENTS:
Bampton pubs and cafés, Aston Pottery, Cogges Farm

ST MARY'S CHURCH

St Mary's Church

Churchgate House

Library

Church View

Bampton Village

Village Hall

Rosemary Lane

Church View

START & END

High Street

Bridge Street

Bampton
Village,
church and
library;
Cogges Manor
Farm and
garden

NEXT PAGE TOP
Cogges Farm near Witney also appeared in *Colette* (2018), about the Nobel-winning French author

NEXT PAGE BOTTOM
The village of Bampton played a starring role in ITV's *Downton Abbey*

ITV's costume drama *Downton Abbey*, depicting the aristocratic lives of the fictional Crawley family in early 20th-century England, was first screened in 2010 and became one of the world's most popular TV shows. Downton is supposedly in Yorkshire, but the village scenes are filmed in Bampton, a pretty Cotswold village fifteen miles (24km) west of Oxford.

Stroll along Bampton's Bridge Street and turn right on a footpath, just before you reach the bridge. Keep straight, with the spire ahead, to emerge on Church View near the **library**. This former school, which became Downton's Cottage Hospital, has a Downton exhibition and sells maps, mugs and memorabilia in a community shop. Turn left to find the handsome **Churchgate House**, which was used for outside shots of Isobel Crawley's house.

Behind the house, **St Mary's Church**, rechristened St Michael and All Angels for Downton, has witnessed several on-screen dramas, including funerals and weddings, as well as Anthony Strallan

(played by Robert Bathurst) jilting Lady Edith (Laura Carmichael) at the altar. Leave the churchyard through the far gate and keep bearing right, around Church Close and Landells, to return to **Church View**, where the old houses double as the Grantham Arms and Lamont's Poultry Merchant.

Keep straight past the library again to see the **cottages** that became the Post Office and the Dog and Duck. The Downton inns may be fictional, but luckily Bampton has several real-life pubs and cafés to choose from. In the neighbouring village of Aston, there is also a lovely tea barn and colourful flower gardens at the pottery.

Cogges Manor Farm in nearby Witney is used as the location for scenes at Yew Tree Farm. Marigold, Lady Edith's illegitimate daughter, lives here in the home of Mr Drewe, a tenant farmer. The **sitting room** walls are decorated with photos of cast and crew and a video about Downton. Next door, there are vintage costumes in the parlour and often welsh cakes cooking on the old-fashioned range

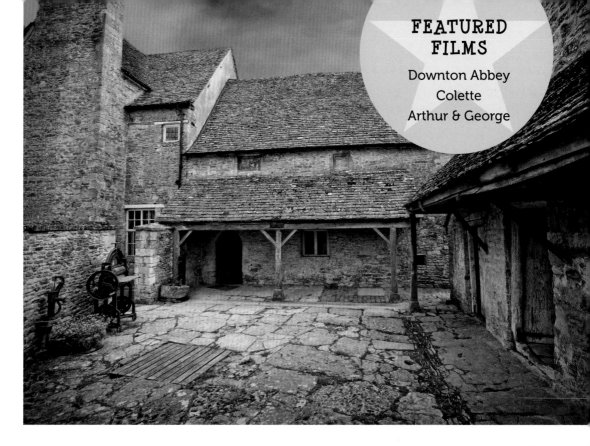

range in the **farmhouse kitchen**. Many scenes were filmed here, but they had to make the spacious kitchen look smaller than it actually is to suit the modest Drewe family. Most of the farm buildings appeared at some point or other during Downton's fifth season.

Step out of the back door into the **vegetable garden**. When the producers of 2018 film *Colette* (starring Keira Knightley and Dominic West) used Cogges as a location, they planted aubergines among the English vegetables to make the garden look more French. The movie charts the writing career and abusive marriage of French novelist and actress Sidonie-Gabrielle Colette, nominated for a Nobel Prize in 1948; her novella *Gigi* became an MGM musical in 1958.

A path from the garden takes you, past the goats, to the pigsties, one of the locations for another ITV costume drama, *Arthur & George* (2015). Based on

the book by Julian Barnes about Sherlock author Arthur Conan Doyle, the cast of the TV series included Martin Clunes, better known as Doc Martin.

Don't miss the atmospheric, beamed tearoom in an old barn and the interesting church nearby.

Further Afield...

Oxfordshire still has plenty more locations for film lovers to explore...

ABOVE Broughton Castle is another popular film location including *Shakespeare in Love*

RIGHT Poster for *Shakespeare in Love*, starring Gwyneth Paltrow as aristocratic would-be actor Viola

Moated **Broughton Castle** near Banbury, with its Tudor architecture, was used to film BBC's *Wolf Hall* (2015), *Jane Eyre* (2011), *Shakespeare in Love* (1998) and *The Madness of King George* (1994), among others.

The old steam trains and engine sheds at **Didcot Railway Centre** appeared in *Anna Karenina* (2012) with Keira Knightley and in *Sherlock Holmes: A Game of Shadows* (2011) starring Robert Downey Jr and Jude Law. They've also been seen in TV series, like *The Camomile Lawn*, *Carrie's War* and the ubiquitous *Inspector Morse*.

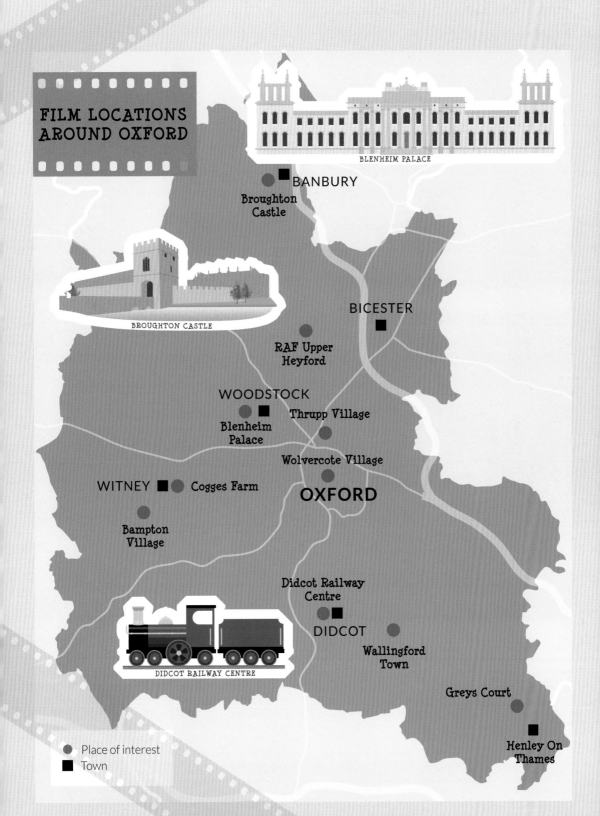

FILM LOCATIONS AROUND OXFORD

BLENHEIM PALACE

BROUGHTON CASTLE

DIDCOT RAILWAY CENTRE

● BANBURY
Broughton Castle

BICESTER

RAF Upper Heyford

WOODSTOCK
Thrupp Village
Blenheim Palace
Wolvercote Village

WITNEY ● Cogges Farm

OXFORD

Bampton Village

Didcot Railway Centre

DIDCOT
Wallingford Town

Greys Court

Henley On Thames

● Place of interest
■ Town

41

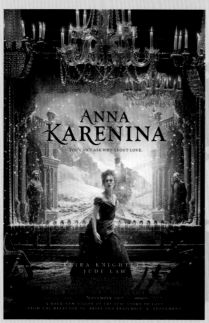

Inspector Morse fans can also follow the famous detective into numerous country pubs, including the pretty, canalside Boat in **Thrupp**, where Morse and Lewis interview the landlord. *Midsomer Murders* was filmed all over South Oxfordshire, with Wallingford and other market towns becoming on-screen Causton. Riverside **Henley-on-Thames** appeared in *The Social Network* (2010) and nearby **Grey's Court** was another location for *Downton Abbey*.

North of Oxford, **RAF Upper Heyford**, now semi-abandoned, appeared in the James Bond film *Octopussy* (1983), *Wonder Woman* (2017) and more. It also became RAF Lower Tadfield, near the fictional, idyllic, childhood home of the antichrist, in the TV adaptation of Neil Gaiman and Terry Pratchett's *Good Omens* (2018). The supernatural series stars Michael Sheen and David Tennant as divine Aziraphale and demonic Crowley, and uses several Oxfordshire locations. The county will doubtless continue to provide future film lovers with scenic adventures for many years to come. Happy exploring!

TOP Didcot Railway Centre has been popular with filmmakers needing a vintage railway

ABOVE Film poster for *Anna Karenina* (2012), starring Keira Knightley, which used Didcot Railway Centre as a location

RIGHT Poster for *Octopussy*, starring Roger Moore as James Bond, which was partly filmed at RAF Upper Heyford in North Oxfordshire

FAR RIGHT Poster for *The Social Network* (2010), which features shots of the famous Henley Royal Regatta

BELOW Henley on Thames also appears in numerous episodes of *Midsomer Murders* as well as other TV series and films

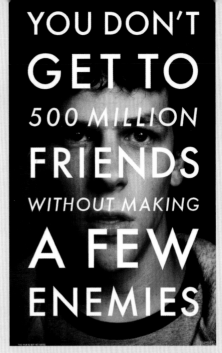

Places to visit

Colleges, University Museums and Churches

Ashmolean Museum
Open 10–5 Tues–Sun, free
01865 278000
www.ashmolean.org

Bodleian Library
Opening times vary
01865 277162
www.bodleian.ox.ac.uk

Botanical Gardens
Open 9–4, £5
01865 286690
www.botanic-garden.ox.ac.uk

Brasenose College
Open 10–11.30am and
    2–4.30pm, £2
01865 277830
www.bnc.ox.ac.uk

Christ Church College
Open 10–4, £8
01865 276150
www.chch.ox.ac.uk

Corpus Christi College
Open free most afternoons
01865 276700
www.ccc.ox.ac.uk

Exeter College
Open free most afternoons
01865 279600
www.exeter.ox.ac.uk

History of Science Museum
Open 12–5 Tues–Sun, free
01865 277280
www.mhs.ox.ac.uk

Keble College
Open 2–5pm, free
01865 272727
www.keble.ox.ac.uk

Lincoln College
Open 2–5pm, free
01865 279800
www.lincoln.ox.ac.uk

Magdalen College
Open most afternoons, £6
01865 276000
www.magd.ox.ac.uk

Mansfield College
Open 9–5 weekdays, free
01865 270999
www.mansfield.ox.ac.uk

Merton College
Open afternoons,
    10–5 weekends, £3
01865 276310
www.merton.ox.ac.uk

Museum of Natural History
Open 10–5, free
01865 272950
www.oum.ox.ac.uk

New College
Open 11–5, £5
01865 279500
www.new.ox.ac.uk

Oriel College
Open 2–5pm, £2
01865 276555
www.oriel.ox.ac.uk

Pitt Rivers Museum
Open 10–4.30, free
01865 270927
www.prm.ox.ac.uk

Sheldonian Theatre
Open 10–4, £3.50
01865 277299
www.admin.ox.ac.uk/sheldonian

St Mary's University Church
Open 9–5 weekdays; 12–5
    Sundays, £4 to climb tower
01865 279111
www.universitychurch.ox.ac.uk

University College
Open 10–4 outside term time, £2
01865 276602
www.univ.ox.ac.uk

University Parks
Open 8–8, free
01865 282040
www.parks.ox.ac.uk

Other places to visit

Aston Pottery
Open 9–5 Mon–Sat; 10.30–5 Sun
01993 852031
www.astonpottery.co.uk

Bampton Library
Open 11–4 Mon–Sat, with a
    lunchbreak; 2–4 Sun
01993 850076
bamptonarchive.org/visit

Blenheim Palace
Open 10.30–5 daily, £25
01993 810530
www.blenheimpalace.com

Cogges Manor Farm
Open 9–5, Mar–Oct, £6.50
01993 772602
www.cogges.org.uk

Oxford Museum
Open 10–5 Mon–Sat, free
 01865 252334
www.oxford.gov.uk/
    museumofoxford

Special thanks to Experience
Oxfordshire for their support.
For further information on
available tours around Oxford,
please visit their website:
www.experienceoxfordshire.org